CONTENTS

KT-499-836

HELLO

Welcome to my guide to some of the tricky issues that may start to become more of a concern for you now that you are getting older. I wrote this book not because I wanted to worry you (or give your parents even more things to worry about), but because I think that knowing about these sorts of things will make you a stronger, wiser and safer person. This can only be a good thing, right? I hope that many of these issues will never affect you at all, but you might have a friend who needs some advice, or a younger brother or sister who really needs your help. This book will help you to help them.

Remember, you never have to go through problems alone. There is ALWAYS someone you can talk to, someone that you can ask for help. But maybe this book will give you a little bit of extra courage to do that, and may give you some idea as to the sorts of things you might say, do, or ask.

Don't let it worry you. I don't know what direction your life is going to take, or what you want to do with yourself, but I do know this: it gets better. And better. And the more you know, the wiser you are, the better it gets. You'll see! ;-)

Good luck,

Dr Christian

YOU ARE WHAT YOU EAT

Your growing body is using lots of energy, which means you will probably feel hungry a lot of the time. Snacking on crisps or chocolate may seem tempting and a quick fix, but your body needs a balanced diet to keep you healthy and feeling great, and sugary foods will quickly make you feel tired and hungry again a short time after eating them.

This food group plate shows us what proportions of food you should eat so that your body gets all the energy and nutrients it needs. Take a look at the boxes opposite to find out how some of the foods you eat are used by your body. Remember, if you are doing lots of sport, exercise or energetic outdoor activities, then your energy requirements will go up. Don't be tempted by silly diets that you may read about in magazines or online, such as 'low carb' – carbohydrates are one of the most important sources of fuel for your body as you grow and are vital to help make your performance in the classroom and in sports as brilliant as possible!

FRUIT AND VEG

— full of the essential vitamins and minerals your body needs to work well. Aim to eat at least five portions a day of fresh, frozen or tinned fruit and veg.

PROTEIN

— meat, eggs, fish and beans all contain protein, which helps you grow.

DAIRY

— foods such as milk, cheese and yoghurt are good sources of calcium, which your body needs to keep your bones and teeth strong.

CARBS

— for energy, you need carbohydrates. You'll find them in bread, rice, potatoes and pasta.

SUGARY, FATTY FOODS

— foods such as cakes, sweets, biscuits and ice cream are high in sugar and fat. Keep them as occasional treats.

DRINKS

— your body needs at least six glasses of water a day. As well as keeping you hydrated, it is great for your skin, hair and teeth. Keep fizzy drinks as occasional treats — the sugar and acid in them can damage your teeth.

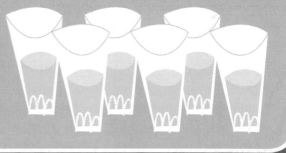

TEETH AND BONES
What you need: vitamin D
Find it in: oily fish, eggs, sunshine
Helps to: keep bones and teeth strong

ENERGY
What you need: vitamin B
Find it in: veg, fruit, wholegrain breads
Helps to: keep muscles healthy, release energy in food

BEING HEALTHY, HEALING
What you need: vitamin C
Find it in: oranges, potatoes, broccoli, peppers, strawberries, blackcurrants
Helps to: protect teeth and gums, keep tissue healthy, heal wounds

GROWTH, EYES, SKIN
What you need: vitamin A
Find it in: milk, eggs, liver, dark leafy veg, orange fruit and veg such as carrots and mangoes
Helps to: keep eyes and skin healthy, keep you growing

MUSCLES AND BLOOD CELLS
What you need: iron
Find it in: red meat, turkey, spinach, beans, nuts, dark leafy veg
Helps to: build muscles, make healthy blood cells

STAYING ACTIVE

Staying healthy and feeling great is not just about eating well. Exercise is important, too. As well as keeping your muscles and bones in top condition, it also releases hormones that make you feel happy and relaxed.

Regular exercise keeps you fit, helps you stay at a healthy weight and it's a great stress-buster. Aim to do at least 30 minutes of activity five times a week.

One of the best ways to make sure you stay fit is by doing something you enjoy. If you don't like PE at school (and I certainly didn't!), remember that there are loads of other things you can do to get you moving.

Varying the activities you do throughout the week will stop you getting bored, too.

FACT FLASH
Make sure you drink water when you are exercising. Staying hydrated helps your body to get the most from your workout.

TRY IT OUT...

Here are just a few activities you may like to try:

STREET DANCE

If you like the idea of freestyle dancing to hip-hop music, give it a try – there are loads of classes out there and many offer free taster sessions.

YOGA

It is a great way to stretch, relax, strengthen your core muscles and learn how to breathe properly.

TRAMPOLINING

This is a brilliant activity to try if you don't like team sports. It strengthens the muscles and is great for balance and co-ordination.

CLIMBING

Many leisure centres have climbing walls – book a trial session to see if you have a head for heights.

MARTIAL ARTS

From karate to judo and kickboxing, there are plenty of martial arts to try.

FENCING

Great for learning attack and defence moves and improving co-ordination.

THE GYM

Many gyms have classes for people aged between 11–16 years, run by a qualified instructor. Weight-bearing exercise is great for your bones and muscles, while cardio workouts help your heart. There are lots of myths and rumours that starting in the gym (especially using the weights) when you are young will stop you growing. They are simply not true. Workouts, if done properly and safely, are safe and good for your growing body and can help keep your weight within the healthy range.

FITNESS FRIENDS

If you don't like the idea of exercising at a club or on a team, there are plenty of other things you can do to stay fit and healthy. Round up a few of your friends and try some of these fun ideas to get your blood pumping.

SKATEBOARDING, SCOOTING, BMXING

Most local parks have ramps that you can use to practise your skateboarding, scooting or BMX skills with your friends.

SUPER CIRCUITS

How about setting up some circuits in your garden or at the local park? Set up several different exercises and take it in turns to do them. Try some of these ideas: skipping, hula hooping, jumping jacks, push ups, shadow boxing, squats. Do each for a minute or two.

DANCE

Put on your favourite tracks and go wild!

CYCLING

Many towns have cycle paths where you can keep fit away from traffic. Find out if there's one near you, get a group together and go out for a spin. Don't forget your helmet!

DOG WALKING

If you have friends or relatives who have a dog, why not volunteer to walk it for them? Take a friend along to chat to and you'll hardly notice that you are exercising.

ICE SKATING

If you have an ice rink nearby, get a group of friends together and get your skates on. Ice skating is a great workout for your legs and, if you keep your speed up, your heart will feel the benefit, too!

Ask Dr Christian

My friend says she's fat...

Q: I'm worried about my best friend. She keeps saying she is fat, even though she's a normal, healthy weight. She constantly talks about calories in food and spends hours looking at pictures of models in magazines, comparing her legs and tummy to theirs. I keep telling her that the images have been photoshopped to make the models look like that but she won't listen. Now she's stopped eating lunch. What can I do to help her?

A: It's very common for girls to worry about their weight from time to time. Some boys do it, too. But it's not good to worry about it ALL the time. This can lead to some really unhealthy eating habits, such as skipping whole meals (like your friend is doing) or even stopping eating altogether. This can be very

dangerous. Maybe your friend is only going to do this for a short time, or this may be the sign of deeper problems and insecurities. If you have serious concerns about her, you should make sure her teacher or parents are aware. Perhaps talk to your school nurse if you have one? You are quite right that most of the images you see in magazines and adverts have been airbrushed and are not realistic images of how women look. I think the fact that you have noticed your friend's issues and are there for her to talk to is the most valuable support of all. Let an adult who knows your friend well help with the rest.

SKIN SENSE

A good diet, plenty of sleep and drinking lots of water are important, but what else do you need to have good skin sense? Here are some top tips to keep your skin looking its best:

SPOTS

Lots of people get spots thanks to sebum – an oil that helps your skin stay waterproof and smooth. It's all due to the changing hormone levels in your body which increase sebum and oil production in your skin, causing spots. If you get an outbreak, don't be tempted to scrub or use lots of harsh skin treatments. It's best to use mild soap twice a day, or use a medicated spot treatment or facial wash. Try to leave the spots alone, as picking or squeezing them will make them last longer and may scar your skin. Avoid foundation and concealer as these may make the acne worse. If you are really unhappy with your skin, ask to see your GP who can offer you a lot of help with treating spots effectively. There is no need to just put up with spots!

ARE YOU NICE TO BE NEAR?

You may have found that you get sweatier in the heat and when you exercise. Perhaps you've also noticed your armpits are a little pongier? This is BO, or body odour. Showering or bathing every day, especially after exercise, and using a deodorant or antiperspirant will make sure that you are nice to be near.

BE SUN SAVVY

Sunshine helps your body make vitamin D, so everyone needs about 15 minutes of sun each day. After that, apply suncream to protect your skin from sunburn. Over time, the UV rays in sunshine can age and damage your skin and even cause skin cancer. Reapply suncream regularly, especially if you are swimming, to protect your skin from UV damage.

Ask Dr Christian

I'm really self-conscious about my spots...

Q: This past year I've been getting spots and in the last few weeks they've got really bad. Now my face is covered in angry red spots! I feel really self-conscious, especially as some people at school have started commenting on it, and I feel like hiding away indoors where no one can see me! My mum says I just need to wait for them to go, but what if they don't? Is there anything I can do to get rid of them forever?

A: Actually there is lots you can do! The first thing to know is that this is not your fault, or anything that you are doing wrong. Spots are not caused by dirt, by your diet or anything else you can control. Sometimes, certain make-ups and skin products can make them worse however, so do ask in the shop you buy them from about this. Your GP has lots of different treatments that they can offer you, from lotions and creams that you put on your skin every day, to stronger pills that can be really effective. They can take some time to work, and sometimes your skin may get a little worse before it gets better, but it will improve with time, so why not ask your parents to make you an appointment with your GP and go have a chat?

STRONG BONES

Your skeleton is the framework that supports you. Your bones work with your muscles to help you move and do everything from running to typing on a keyboard. At the moment, your body and your bones are still growing, so it is extra important that you make sure your bones get everything they need to stay strong and healthy.

EXERCISE

Make sure you get plenty of exercise – this helps to strengthen your bones. Things such as running, skipping and carrying things – 'weight-bearing exercises' – are the best way to strengthen your bones. Try to maintain a healthy weight, too, as being over or underweight can affect your bone health when you are older.

EAT WELL

Milk, cheese, yoghurt, dark leafy veg, beans and tinned fish are all good sources of calcium – a mineral your bones need to stay healthy. Try to drink water and avoid fizzy drinks, which can make it harder for your body to absorb calcium.

SUNSHINE

Your body also needs vitamin D from sunshine to help your bones use calcium from food. Make sure you get around 15 minutes of sun every day.

GROWING PAINS

Have you ever had an achey feeling in your legs? This may be what is known as 'growing pains'. They happen because your bones grow slightly faster than your muscles, which makes them ache as they stretch. Growing pains are perfectly normal and usually don't need treatment.

FACT FLASH

As we age, our bones become weaker. This tends to affect girls more than boys. Building strong, healthy bones now will help guard against bone issues when you are older.

HEALTHY HAIR

You may have noticed that, like your skin, your hair feels more greasy. This is because the oil (or sebum) that your skin produces is also produced by your hair follicles. Using harsh shampoos won't stop your hair from getting greasy and it can make it worse. If you do feel that you need to wash your hair every day, use a mild shampoo. If you have long hair, add a small dab of conditioner to the ends to protect them.

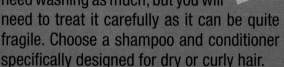

CARING FOR CURLS

Usually, curly hair is drier than straight hair. It probably doesn't need washing as much, but you will need to treat it carefully as it can be quite fragile. Choose a shampoo and conditioner specifically designed for dry or curly hair.

HAIR AND SPOTS

If you have spots, it's a good idea to keep your hair off your face, as the oil from it may cause blocked pores and aggravate existing spots.

BEAT THE HEAT

From hairdryers to straighteners and curling irons to heated styling brushes, there are lots of ways to style your hair. But they all involve heat, which can damage your hair. There are lots of styling sprays and products to protect your hair when you are heat styling – but even so, try not to do it every day.

FLAKY!

If you are wearing a dark top and you notice white flakes on your shoulders, you might have dandruff. These are flakes of dead skin. It's not harmful, but it can make you feel self-conscious. Use an anti-dandruff shampoo and, if it doesn't clear up, your doctor may be able to help you.

CRAZY COLOUR

There are many ways to colour your hair, from henna to wash-in, wash-out temporary colours through to permanent ones that have to grow out. Permanent and semi-permanent colours can damage the condition of your hair. It's also important to do a skin test 48 hours before you use them to make sure you are not allergic to the dye.

MOUTH MATTERS

Fresh breath and lovely clean teeth can make you feel really good about yourself. Flashing a sparkling smile can also put others at ease and make you seem confident and friendly. But did you know that there are plenty of other reasons why looking after your teeth is a good idea?

By the time you are an adult, you will have 32 teeth, including four wisdom teeth. Your teeth have to last you a lifetime, so it is sensible to look after them well. Getting into good habits now can save a lot of pain and time in the dentist's chair later! Regular six-monthly check-ups with your dentist will keep your teeth in great shape and make sure that any problems are picked up and treated quickly, before they become serious. If you have any questions about caring for your teeth, your dentist will be able to help you.

BRUSHING

Care of your teeth starts with brushing. Choose a small or medium head toothbrush and a toothpaste containing at least 1,350ppm (parts per million) of fluoride. Brush your teeth every morning and evening for two minutes each time.

FLOSSING

Use dental floss or interdental sticks to get rid of trapped food and plaque (the yellow gunk on your teeth that's full of bacteria). This will help to keep your gums healthy and your breath fresh.

CAVITIES

Plaque on your teeth is full of bacteria that produce acid. This eats away at the hard enamel coating on your teeth, making a hole, or cavity. Cleaning away the plaque helps to prevent cavities. It's best to try to prevent them happening – keep sweets and sugary drinks as occasional treats and brush, brush, brush!

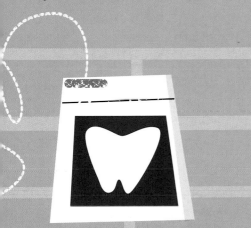

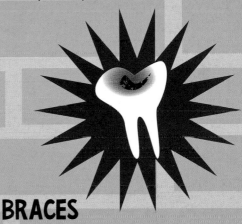

FRESH BREATH

Bad breath can usually be sorted with regular brushing, flossing and using a mouthwash. But sometimes it can be down to an infection or an allergy. See your dentist first, and if he or she can't find a cause, make an appointment with your doctor.

BRACES

If your adult teeth are a bit crooked you may need a brace. This could be a removable one called a retainer, or you may be offered fixed braces known as train tracks. Braces may feel strange at first, but you will get used to them. Remember that it's not forever and you will have beautiful, straight teeth afterwards. Make sure you keep your braces and teeth clean – your orthodontist will show you how to look after them – as trapped food can cause cavities.

BRIGHT EYES

Our eyes are our window on the world. The muscles in our eyes work faster than any others in the body and make thousands of tiny movements every day, so it makes sense to take care of them. You can help to keep your eyes healthy by getting regular exercise and eating a balanced diet. Most people know that carrots are good for eye health, but eating leafy greens, apricots, eggs, oranges, tomatoes and green beans is also important if you want to look after your sight.

TOP EYE TIPS

- Headaches or struggling to read the board at school can be a sign that your eyesight has changed. Pop along to your optician for a check-up.

- Make sure you get enough sleep, because your eyes won't be at their best if they are tired.

- Don't spend too long staring at a TV screen, computer or tablet without a break. The glare can strain your eyes and it can also make your eyes dry and tired.

- Regular eye tests at an optician are also important to make sure your eyes are healthy.

- If you are playing badminton or squash, doing science experiments, or helping your parents with some DIY, make sure you protect your eyes from injury with safety glasses or goggles.

If your optometrist tells you that you need glasses, how do you weigh up what's best? Should you try contact lenses? If so, which type? There's no right or wrong answer. The best thing to do is to find out what works best for you. There is a huge amount of choice in glasses and in contact lenses, but to get you started here are a few pros and cons about each:

GLASSES

Pros: There are some great frames out there, and the geeky look is very on-trend. Glasses don't touch the eye so anyone can wear them. They are fairly cheap to replace and you can often get deals where you get two pairs for the price of one. They're easier to care for than contact lenses.

Cons: Easy to forget, lose or break. They steam up in the rain or cold weather. You can't wear them for some sports, such as swimming. They can also be uncomfortable in hot weather.

CONTACT LENSES

Pros: You don't look any different when wearing them – most people won't know they are there! Once you get used to them and they are in, you can forget about them. They don't fog up like glasses and it is easier to wear protective goggles for sport with contact lenses in. Daily disposable lenses do not need cleaning fluids.

Cons: More expensive than glasses. Some lenses need careful daily cleaning. Good hand hygiene is also important to avoid transferring germs to the eyes. If your prescription is quite strong, you may still need glasses as well when you take lenses out at night.

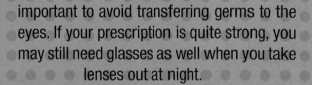

FACT FLASH
Laser surgery can permanently correct eyesight problems. But it is expensive, and shouldn't be considered until your late teens when you've stopped growing, as your eyesight may still be changing.

HEALTHY HEARING

Like eyesight, your hearing is one of your most important senses. Whether you are listening to your favourite music or hanging out chatting with your mates, if your hearing isn't in good shape you will be missing out. Here's what you need to know to make sure you have healthy hearing:

From the quietest whisper to the roar of a jet engine, your ears are able to hear an amazing range of noises. Sound waves shake the eardrum – tiny hairs deep inside the ear detect these movements and your brain interprets them as sound. Fluid-filled tubes deep in your ears also help you to balance. Like your eyes, your ears are very complex, delicate parts of your body so it is important to look after them.

HANDLE WITH CARE

If your ears are painful, it's best to see your doctor. Don't be tempted to poke about in your ears, as it is easy to damage the eardrum. Cotton buds should never be inserted in the ear canal – it can push earwax against the eardrum, making it very painful and hard to hear.

EAR BUDS

Listening to music is great, especially when you can play it through your phone or MP3 player. Watch the volume though. If other people can hear your music when you are wearing headphones, the chances are it is too loud. A good rule of thumb is 60/60 – the volume of your player should be around or lower than 60% of the maximum and you should try to limit your listening time to no more than 60 minutes at a time. Big headphones are fashionable at the moment and these tend to be better for your ear health than ear buds. If you notice a loud ringing in your ears, you may have tinnitus. This can happen temporarily after a loud concert or noise. If it continues, see your doctor.

EAR PIERCINGS

From lobes to cartilage and tragus, and from rooks all the way through to tunnels – the piercing possibilities for ears are endless. The chances are that you will be starting with a simple lobe piercing. Here's what you need to know:

● Pick somewhere reputable to have them done. If you are under 16, most piercing places will want permission from a parent or guardian.

● Lobe piercings should be done with earrings taken from a sealed, sterile pack. The piercer will probably use a 'gun' to insert the earrings. It is over in seconds, but your ear may feel numb and hot for a while.

● You'll need to keep the studs in for six weeks to allow the ears to heal.

● Keep the holes clean – wash your hands and mix up ¼ tsp of sea salt with an egg cup full of warm water. Dip a cotton bud into the solution and rub it on the front and back of the ear lobe, gently turning the earrings so that the saline gets into the hole.

● If your ear gets red and angry-looking, or if it is hot, you may have an infection. See your doctor, who will probably advise you to leave the piercing in to help the infection drain. You may be given antibiotic cream or tablets to clear it up.

FACT FLASH

Bored of your piercing? Most can be removed and usually the holes will close up over time – but be aware that using large tunnels to stretch your lobes can be permanent, so think carefully before you do it.

21

GET WELL SOON...

ACHES, PAINS AND LURGIES

From coughs and colds to vomiting and earache, the chances are that at some point you have had these common illnesses. Usually, they are easy to treat at home and will clear up quite quickly. So what causes them and how can you get rid of them?

VOMITING AND DIARRHOEA

Most germs that cause upset stomachs are passed on when someone doesn't wash their hands after they go to the toilet. The germs on their hands get on everything they touch – from door handles to food (yuck!). If the germs get into your body, it will get rid of them by emptying your stomach and bowels. At the time it can make you feel awful and, as well as the vomiting and diarrhoea, you may have a headache and a temperature. Usually it is enough to rest and take small, frequent sips of water and you will feel better after a couple of days, although it can take a week or longer to feel 100% again. If you are ill, make sure you stay off school until 48

hours after your last bout of sickness or diarrhoea so that you don't pass it on to others. Always wash your hands well with soap and hot water when you use the toilet and before you prepare food.

HEADACHES

There are lots of things that can cause headaches. Mostly it is something really simple, like not drinking enough water, changes in your eyesight, or being hungry, tired or upset. You may also get a headache if you have a cold. Usually headaches are nothing to worry about. Drink plenty of water and have a lie down in a quiet place if need be and it should pass. If it doesn't, you can speak to your parent and they may give you a painkiller such as paracetamol. If you find you get headaches regularly, take a look at your diet. The caffeine in chocolate and energy drinks can cause headaches, so try cutting them out for a while to see if it makes a difference.

TONSILLITIS

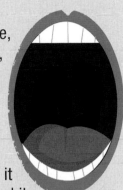

A sore throat, headache, pain when you swallow, fever and swollen, aching glands in your neck... If you've ever had these symptoms then you may have had tonsillitis. Usually it is caused by a virus and it will get better in a few days if you rest, drink plenty of fluids and take painkillers. If your doctor thinks that your tonsillitis is caused by a bacterial infection he or she may give you antibiotics. Make sure you follow the instructions on your medicine and always finish it, even if you start to feel better.

TUMMY ACHE

A tummy ache without vomiting or diarrhoea is usually caused by something as simple as constipation – when your poo becomes hard and it is painful going to the toilet. Increasing the amount of water you drink and eating more fibre can help with this. If you really are struggling to poo, see your doctor who may recommend taking a laxative to soften your poo. Laxatives should only be taken for a few days and are no substitute for having a good diet, drinking water and getting regular exercise.

Another cause of tummy pain can be trapped wind (or flatulence). This can be caused by eating foods that produce gas when they are digested, such as baked beans. If gas builds up it can make you feel bloated or even cause pain. Gentle exercise, a hot-water bottle on your tummy, or drinking peppermint tea can help to relieve it.

PERIOD PAIN

Some women describe period pain as 'cramps' or a 'dragging ache' in the lower abdomen. This usually only lasts a day or so at the beginning of your period and will be quite mild. Putting a hot water bottle on your lower back or tummy can relieve the pain, or you could try a soak in a warm bath. You may not feel like exercising, but going for a walk can really ease things. Take a look at your diet, too. Make sure you are eating healthily and drinking plenty of water.

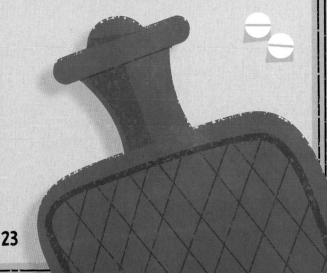

ASTHMA AND OTHER IRRITATIONS

Allergies, asthma and hay fever can be annoying if they stop you doing things you enjoy. But you can do a lot to manage these conditions, especially if you know what triggers them and how to deal with symptoms.

HAY FEVER

Most of us enjoy spring and summer, but if you have hay fever you might not be quite as keen. Hay fever is caused by a sensitivity to the pollen made by grass, trees or plants. It causes itchy, swollen eyes, sneezing and a runny nose. You can check the pollen count on weather forecast sites. On 'high' days, it's best to wear wrap-around sunglasses to stop the pollen getting in your eyes. If you've been outside, showering and changing your clothes can get rid of the pollen. Your GP may also suggest you get an antihistamine from the chemist, which can help to relieve symptoms, and eye drops and nose sprays can also help. Don't be shy about asking for treatment – there is nothing more miserable than having each summer spoiled by hay fever, but with the right treatments, it can be well controlled.

ALLERGIES

People can be allergic to all sorts of things, from nuts, milk or wheat, to wasp and bee stings and even the latex in balloons! Many people with allergies are diagnosed at a young age, but if you have just been diagnosed, don't panic. The most important thing is to make sure you know as much as you can about your allergy. Your doctor will be able to advise you on what to avoid and, if it is a food allergy, how to make sure you eat a balanced diet while avoiding trigger foods. You will also need advice about how to read food labels, what to do when you are eating out and how to cope when you are away from home. If you have a life-threatening allergy, such as to nuts or stings, you may be given a special pen that injects medicine if you need it fast. Make sure that you carry it with you and that you and your family know how to use it in an emergency.

ASTHMA

Asthma is caused by inflammation of the tubes that take air in and out of the lungs. It can be triggered by all sorts of things, such as dust mites, smoke, food allergies, illness, damp and mould and even exercise. If you are diagnosed with asthma it is important to know what your triggers are and what to do. Make sure you carry your blue reliever inhaler with you and, if you have a preventer inhaler, take it regularly even when you are feeling well. If you are wheezing, coughing, tight-chested or breathless, you may be having an asthma attack. Take your reliever inhaler and, if your symptoms do not improve, you must contact your doctor. If your reliever inhaler isn't helping at all and you are struggling to talk, your fingernails are blue and your pulse is racing, you may be having a serious asthma attack – call 999.

ECZEMA

Eczema is patches of itchy, dry skin that may become cracked and very sore. There are lots of different types of eczema and it can be triggered by anything from pollen to food allergies or even a reaction to harsh soaps and laundry detergents. Usually eczema flares up on the inside of the elbows, the back of the knees, around the eyes and ears or the neck. It is treated with special moisturisers called emollients. If a bad flare-up occurs, your doctor may prescribe a cream to help the skin heal. Make sure you apply your emollients every day and keep your nails short. If you have a flare-up, try not to scratch as the eczema may get infected.

FACT FLASH

If you are diagnosed with asthma, ask your doctor for an Asthma Action Plan. It tells you exactly how to manage your condition and what to do if you are having an attack.

KEEPING FEET SWEET

Everyone gets sweaty feet now and then. So how do you make sure your trainers don't give off any nasty niffs and your toenails are in tip-top condition? Here's how to keep your feet sweet...

TOP TOES

Every day, wash your feet in hot, soapy water and put on a clean pair of cotton socks. This will help keep the nasty niffs at bay! The best time to cut your toenails is just after a bath or shower, as the nails will be nice and soft. Using clippers, cut straight across your toenails. Make sure you don't leave any sharp points as this can cause painful ingrown toenails.

VERRUCAS

Verrucas are warts that grow on the soles of the feet and get pushed into your feet because you walk on them all day. They can be quite painful. You can pick them up from walking barefoot around swimming pools or changing rooms. They can be treated by painting chemicals on them or by freezing them off, and you can get products to do this from the chemist. If they are not causing you any problems, you can leave them alone and they should go on their own eventually.

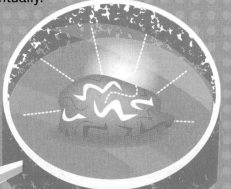

SPRAINS AND STRAINS

If you sprain your ankle, you should Rest it, apply Ice, Compression and Elevate it (RICE for short).

HEEL HELL

High heels force your feet forward, squashing your toes. They also put pressure on your back, knees and ankles. It's best to keep heels for special occasions only – your feet will thank you for it.

Ask Dr Christian

I've got itchy, smelly feet...

Q: My feet smell terrible, and my toes are really itchy! What should I do?

A: This sounds like you have a very common problem called athlete's foot. It is caused by a fungal infection in your skin that is often caused by the skin of your feet being wet or sweaty. There is probably plenty of the fungus that causes athlete's foot on the floor of your changing room at school, and this may be where you picked it up from. It is really easy to treat with some anti-fungal cream that you should rub all over both feet twice a day for at least 7 days. Change your socks every day and, if your shoes or trainers are really old and stinky, see if you can get a new pair. You can also get anti-fungal foot powder that you put in your shoes to help stop the problem coming back.

CUTS

Small, shallow cuts usually just need a plaster. First wash your hands – you don't want to get any germs in the wound! Dry your hands thoroughly, then rinse the wound under lukewarm water. Pat it dry with a clean towel and, if it is still bleeding, press  the cloth gently on the wound until it has stopped. Apply some antiseptic cream, then cover it with a plaster. If blood seeps through the plaster, or you are worried that the cut has something in it (such as dirt or gravel) ask an adult for help.

MINOR BURNS

The most important thing with a burn is to act fast. Run the tap until the water is cool, but not ice cold. Place the burn under running water for at least 15 minutes. If the burn  is to your leg or foot, you can use the bath tap or shower instead. If the skin is broken, or the burn is bigger than a postage stamp, ask an adult for help as it may need medical treatment.

STINGS

Bee stings and wasp stings are a real pain in summer. If you are stung by a bee, you may need to remove the sting. Because it has little hooks which can break off and get stuck, you must never pull a sting out. You can remove it safely using a ruler or a plastic card to scrape across the surface of the skin to ease the sting out. Then wash the area with soap and water and pat it dry. A cool flannel or towel with ice inside over the sting can ease the pain and swelling.

Ask Dr Christian

I'm too embarrassed to talk to my GP...

Q: How do I bring up embarrassing stuff with my doctor? I'm worried she might laugh...

A: I'll be honest with you; your doctor is far too busy to laugh. They probably have another five people to see just in the same hour that you are there! Also remember that whilst your problem might be a first for you, it most definitely won't be for your doctor. Even the most personal problem quickly stops being funny for us doctors when you have seen it a few hundred times! Doctors train for more than six years, not so that they can laugh at you, but so they can help you and make you better. Go and have a chat if you are worried about anything – I promise it won't be as bad as you think.

DRINK AND DRUGS

Although it isn't legal to drink alcohol until you are 18, you might come into contact with it before then. Alcohol, cigarettes and legal highs can be dangerous, so it's important you know the facts.

BOOZE BASICS

When adults socialize, alcohol is often available. People drink it at celebrations, to relax at the end of a hard week, or even just when they are having a nice meal.

If people drink too much, it can affect their judgement and co-ordination. This means they may do embarrassing or risky things that they wouldn't dream of doing if they hadn't had a drink. Too much drink in one go can make you sick or even make you pass out, which can be very dangerous. Many young people have died from drinking too much alcohol, and I would call it one of our most dangerous legal highs.

SMOKING

Although cigarettes are legal if you are over 18 years of age, they are very harmful. Smoking is bad for your body. It damages your lungs, can cause many different types of cancer, ages the skin and also makes your skin and clothes smell bad.

'Vaping' is a form of smoking that uses an electronic cigarette to produce a vapour containing nicotine. Often the vapour is fruit-flavoured, but this doesn't mean they are healthy. E-cigarettes are relatively new and, whilst I think they are very helpful at getting people to stop smoking cigarettes, they are certainly not something to start doing if you don't already smoke.

DRUGS AND LEGAL HIGHS

There are many illegal drugs around, such as cannabis (marijuana/dope/weed), amphetamines (speed), methamphetamine (meth), ecstasy (E), ketamine (K), cocaine (coke), heroin (H) and crack cocaine. They can be very addictive and, because they are illegal, you have no way of knowing what is in them or how strong they are. Some drugs are mixed with all sorts of things such as glass or brick dust!

Some drugs aren't currently illegal, but may be just as dangerous. People might try and persuade you to try them, but just because 'legal highs' are legal doesn't mean they are safe. In fact, the only way they can be sold is if they are labelled as something else like plant food or bath salts. Some people have even died the first time they tried them. Bottom line... don't be fooled into thinking these are safe to take. For more info, see the Resources section on page 92.

Ask Dr Christian

My friend is trying to make me drink alcohol...

Q: A group of us hang around together at the park. Some of the older kids bring drink with them. My friend has been drinking for the past few weeks with them and now she keeps hassling me to. I tried it but I don't like the taste. Should I drink anyway so my friend still likes me?

A: I think you have to ask yourself why your friend is trying to make you do something that you don't want to do. Is it to make herself feel better about the fact that she is drinking and knows that she shouldn't be? I suspect so. You should make it clear to your friend that you don't want to be doing this with her and that you are going to stay away from her each time she goes off to the park to drink. If she decides not to be your friend any more then I think you have been the lucky one, and she has lost a kind and concerned friend.

ONLINE SAFETY

NET KNOW-HOW

As a doctor I'm a huge fan of the internet. I like my patients to look things up before they come and see me, or after I have diagnosed them with something. And I can always look up information to check that I have got things right, or even when I have absolutely no idea and need a little extra help! The internet can be a wonderful place for fun and entertainment, learning and discovery. It's packed with information and helps people to stay connected. You can download music, videos, watch films and play games. The downside is that there is lots of incorrect information as well. Some websites will deliberately try to mislead you, or to sell you products that don't work or are harmful. Some websites may try to take your money without selling you anything at all. And, just like in the real world, people are lurking online who may try to take advantage of you. Some people even make completely fake online identities for themselves in order to con, mislead and harm others. Here are some of my tips to help keep you safe when you are surfing:

- Think about your internet footprint. Whatever you post on the internet is usually there forever. A good rule is to ask yourself whether you would be happy to send the photograph or what you have written on a postcard to your friends and family. If it would make you cringe, then don't do it! Remember it may not just be your friends who look at your Facebook page — your mum or your teachers may look at it too…

- On social networking sites and chat forums, it's best to make up a false name rather than using your real one. Your profile picture on many sites will be public, no matter how careful you are with your privacy settings. You don't have to use a picture of you for your profile. It's safer to choose something 'anonymous' like an object or a symbol.

- Learn to use the privacy settings on a site. Make sure that you set your profile so that only people you are friends with can see what you are posting.

- If you leave a site, deactivate or delete your account. This will stop it being hacked without you knowing.

- Keep your personal details private and remember that the gorgeous '14-year-old' you have been chatting to may in fact be an adult with a fake profile. It's easy to set these up and pretend to be someone else

in order to gain someone's trust and before you know it, they've got enough information from your chats to be able to work out where you live, go to school and much more.

- Choose a strong password with letters, numbers and symbols and don't share it with anyone else — not even your best friend! It's a good idea to change your password every so often and make sure that you have different ones for your email and other accounts.

- If you like gaming and play online, keep your full name, address and mobile number to yourself. If a user makes you feel uncomfortable, learn how to mute, block or delete them, and don't be afraid to do so.

- A blog is a great way to talk about things that are happening in your life, or a hobby you do. Again, make sure you don't give too much away — be vague about where you live and don't post your real name or pictures of you and your friends in school uniform.

- If you are having a party or a get-together with your friends, think carefully about sharing it on a social networking site. If you accidentally set your invite to 'public', rather than just selecting the friends you want to invite, you may find your low-key gathering has turned into the party of the decade with a few hundred unwanted extras!

TROLL TROUBLE

The downside to the internet is that, because it is anonymous, it allows people to create an online personality that may be very different to who they are in real life. Hiding behind a computer screen allows people to say and do things that they would never dream of doing in the real world. People who are nasty to others on the internet are known as 'trolls' or 'cyber-bullies'.

LOST IN TRANSLATION

It's easy for things to be taken the wrong way online – someone may think you are being nasty when that wasn't your intention at all. However, trolls like to deliberately stir up trouble by posting something nasty then sitting back and watching the drama as it unfolds.

WHY DO PEOPLE TROLL?

People troll for all sorts of reasons: boredom, loneliness or for power or attention. It also gives them a chance to say things they would never say face-to-face. Online they don't have to justify or explain it – and often they will walk away once they feel they've upset people.

HOW TO DEAL WITH TROLLS

The simplest way to deal with a troll is to ignore what they've posted. Don't be tempted to try to reason or argue with them. If they don't get a reaction they'll probably get bored and go somewhere else instead.

There are different types of cyber-bullying that people may use to try and threaten or frighten you online. They are just as harmful as real-life bullying and just as serious. In fact, cyber-bullying is against the law. Here are some of the main forms of cyber-bullying:

MALICIOUS MAIL

Nasty or threatening email messages. Emails may be copied to groups of people to try and get them to join in with the bullying.

MESSAGING

Sending unpleasant comments via text or by instant messages. Again these may be sent to a wider group of people to try and encourage others to join in.

SOCIAL MEDIA

Setting up fake profiles to tease or bully someone. Posting nasty or threatening comments or embarrassing pictures to their profile or someone else's to upset them.

SMARTPHONES

Sending horrible text messages, making threatening phone calls or sending photos or videos to humiliate or embarrass someone.

PRETENDING TO BE THE PERSON

Setting up profiles, email accounts or making blog entries or posting photos and videos in someone else's name to make fun of someone, threaten them or embarrass them.

BEAT THE BULLIES:

If someone posts something really nasty or is regularly causing trouble on sites you use, it can make you feel very upset and scared, particularly as the bullying can 'follow' you wherever you go, thanks to mobile phones making internet access so easy. Don't be afraid to tell someone. If you can, tell an adult such as a parent or a teacher and they will be able to help you deal with the problem – often it's useful to take screenshots of any posts as evidence. Many popular social media sites and gaming sites have ways of reporting trolls and cyber-bullies – make sure you know what to do. You can also block or delete bullies from your profile so they can't communicate with you.

TROLLS, CYBER-BULLYING AND THE LAW

It is possible for IT experts to trace trolls, and in some really nasty cases, they have been identified by the police and prosecuted.

Ask Dr Christian

He wants me to send him photos...

Q: I've been messaging a guy online for a while now, but he's started to threaten me. He wants me to send him photos and says if I don't he knows where I live. He's really scared me, but my parents will go mad if they find out. How can I fix this?

A: I'm sure you must be very scared about all this. It really is not something you should be dealing with on your own; you must tell someone about this. It's very important. This sort of bullying behaviour is not acceptable and is, in many cases, illegal. I don't think your parents will be mad at you if you tell them about it. In fact I think it is important that you do tell them. They will be concerned but they will be able to help you and can talk to the police for you if they think it necessary. You must stop contacting this person completely from now on and if they do try to contact you in any other way then make sure your parents and teachers know all about it. Remember, never give out any personal details to people online. Just like you would never talk to or go off with strangers on the street, neither should you chat to strangers online.

Ask Dr Christian

I feel so used...

Q: I post on a chat forum for teens. For the last few months a girl has been confiding in us all. She has loads of problems so we've spent hours listening to her and trying to help her out. I've been really worried about her – even losing sleep over it. But last night we found out she's a troll who was just looking for attention. I feel so used! How do I avoid being fooled like this again?

A: As you have learned, it can be very difficult to work out who is real and who is fake online. You were doing the right thing by trying to help someone you thought was upset and in distress. The fact that she was just wasting your time is very annoying. But I don't think it should put you off the internet. It will just help you to understand the various ways in which people look for attention. Perhaps she really was lonely and upset, and even if her stories were not true, your attention did something to help her. But generally I suggest that you spend your time and energy helping real friends – friends you know and have met in person – and keep your internet buddies for lighter chat. If they start mentioning problems, then suggest that they share these with their own friends and family.

STRANGER SAVVY

One night, you are sitting with your mates watching a film when a complete stranger walks into your room. He sits down beside you, makes himself comfy and starts nicking your popcorn. You'd be quite shocked if this happened, wouldn't you? It may not happen in real life, but on the internet it's very easy for a stranger to wander in without being invited. Here's how to stay stranger savvy online:

SO MUCH IN COMMON

It's easy for someone to find out loads about you online, especially if you leave your profile settings public. In a few clicks, it's possible to find out where you go to school, what your favourite TV programmes and films are, which bands you listen to, even the exact location of your house. Be savvy and keep your profile set to private so only friends can see it.

WHO ARE YOUR FRIENDS?

Think about your instant messaging or your social networking pages. How many people on there are people you know well in real-life? It's easy to be tempted to add as many people as you can to try and look popular, but don't just add anyone and everyone to your list. Keep your instant messenger code private and only share it with close friends.

FEELING UNCOMFORTABLE

Imagine that you are on one of your favourite sites. You've been chatting to someone for a while. Amazingly, they like all the same bands, TV shows, films and hobbies as you do! You feel so relaxed chatting to them and you feel like you can tell them things that even your real-life best friend doesn't know. Before you know it, even though you haven't known your online friend long, you have shared some of your deepest secrets with them. Then, out of the blue, your new online 'friend' starts being weird. They start saying things that make you feel really uncomfortable. They have also started to threaten you if you don't do what they say. You feel trapped – you know you have been stupid to trust this person but it feels like it is too late. You don't want everyone to know the secrets you told your 'friend' and it seems that there's no way out and you will have to do what they say...

Being bullied into doing something is very scary and is something you shouldn't have to deal with on your own. The best thing to do is to take screenshots of everything that has been said, then delete the person from your friend list and block them. Make sure you tell a parent or a teacher about what has happened, too. You won't be in trouble and they will be able to help you deal with it safely. Many sites have a button you can use to report someone – you can find out more about online safety at: www.thinkuknow.co.uk.

Ask Dr Christian

My friend has started saying weird things...

Q: I met a boy in a chat room and we've been texting for months but recently he's started saying stuff that makes me a bit uncomfortable. I don't want to lose him as a friend, so how should I handle it?

A: First I would tell him when he says something that makes you uncomfortable and ask him not to talk about those sorts of things. Then see what his reaction is. If he gets annoyed or ignores your request and continues to make these sorts of comments, then perhaps he is not the person you thought he was. I would warn him that if he continues you will stop communicating with him. Unfortunately this may be exactly what you need to do if he persists. It may seem sad to lose a friend, but perhaps he never really intended to be your friend, and had some very different, possibly even nasty, motives.

Ask Dr Christian

A girl I met online wants to meet up...

Q: I've been chatting to a girl the same age as me online. We've been making plans to meet up. Last night she messaged me to say that she can't meet me off the train so her dad will pick me up instead. I've known her for months and I trust her, so it should be OK to go, shouldn't it?

A: No, it really is most certainly not. Look at it this way: you are basically agreeing to meet a man much older than you who you have never met, never spoken to and know nothing about. Does this sound sensible? I'm sorry to say it but it may be that it is actually this man that you have been chatting to all this time, and not a girl at all. The man has been pretending to be someone else and just waiting for the right moment to win your trust and then meet you. It is scary, I know, but you must always be suspicious of these sorts of things happening. Because of these sorts of people, I strongly suggest that if you go anywhere to meet anyone for the first time then you should take an adult with you to make sure that all is ok. You may be very grateful you did if things don't go to plan.

GET THE PICTURE

One of the beauties of smartphones is that it means you have a camera with you wherever you go. You can snap and share pictures throughout your day – everything from selfies to what you had for lunch. It means that almost everything you experience can be shared online, but this isn't without its downsides. Remember that photos are the same as everything else you post on the internet. Once it is up there, it's there for good...

DO ask yourself if you would be happy for a photo to be put on a billboard for all your friends and family to see. If the answer is no, think twice about posting it!

DO remember that photos stay online forever. What does the picture you are posting say about you? Would you be happy for it to pop up again when you are older?

DO remember to switch OFF your location services on your photos. You can do this in your phone settings. If you leave them on, people can click on photos and see exactly where they were taken, which could give them your home address and school.

DO think before you post embarrassing or unflattering photos of your friends. Ask yourself if you would be happy if they did the same to you. If the answer is no, think again!

DO think about where your webcam is. It's rare but they can be hacked and pictures taken without people knowing. Turn it off, cover it or shut your laptop when it's not in use.

SEXTING

Sexting is when a person sends someone else a photo or video of themselves partially or totally naked, or a text talking about sex in a very graphic way. Some people find it very exciting and it is perfectly legal if you are over the age of 18 and the person you are sharing it with is too.

The thing to remember about sexting is that, even if you are over 18 and happy to send the picture, once you press send, you have no idea where the image, text or video could end up! Often a person will sext someone who has promised they won't show anyone else, only to find that they were lying and they've sent it to everyone or worse still, posted it online. So before you share a photo, ask yourself if you would be happy for it to be printed as a flyer and pasted all over town. No? Then press delete, not send!

THE LAW

You and your friends have been having a giggle over a naked picture one of the year 9s sent his girlfriend. He's mortified, but you and your friends think it's just a bit of harmless fun. The trouble is that anyone who takes, possesses or sends naked or sexual photos of a person who is under 18 years old is breaking the law – even if the image is of themselves.

BLINK AND YOU'LL MISS IT...

Some apps allow you to send photos that appear on the screen for seconds before being deleted. But don't be fooled into thinking this is a 'safe' way to send stuff. If someone is quick, they can take a screenshot, which means your message or photo may be more permanent than you hoped...

WHAT TO DO

If someone is pressurizing you into doing something you feel uncomfortable about, don't be scared to say no and tell someone you trust. You won't be in trouble – the people who care about you are there to keep you safe and look after you. They can help you report it, block the person and report them to the police.

STAYING SAFE (IN THE REAL WORLD)

STREETWISE SKILLS

Becoming more independent and taking responsibility is a big part of growing up. The chances are that you have already started going out and about on your own, but even if you don't do it much yet, it's important to know what to do, especially if you are about to start secondary school.

There are lots of things you can do to keep safe when you are out and about…

FACT FLASH
Always trust your instincts. If something or someone is making you feel uneasy, stay calm. Make your way to the nearest busy place, such as a shop, library or café, and ask an adult to help you.

BUSY IS BEST
Choose your route with care and stick to busy, well-lit streets.

STICK TOGETHER
If you can, try to go out with a friend or in a group.

44

BE SAFE

Don't take shortcuts down alleys or lonely paths, even if you are in a rush.

STAY ALERT

Listening to music is great, but when you are out and about, it's best to take your headphones off so you know what's going on around you. This is especially important if you are cycling or crossing the road.

STRANGERS

Never, ever go off with a stranger, no matter how convincing they are. Even if someone you know says your parents have asked them to collect you, don't take their word for it – call your parents and check.

CURFEWS

If your parents allow you to stay out late but expect you in at a certain time, try to stick to it. If you think you'll be late, call or text them. It takes seconds and is much better than getting home to angry parents. It also shows your parents that they can trust you, which means they are more likely to say yes the next time you ask to do something new.

BEING FOLLOWED?

If you think that someone might be following you, cross the road carefully or head to the nearest busy place.

45

TRAVEL TIPS

Travelling somewhere new on your own may seem quite daunting, particularly if you're used to going with your parents or friends. There are lots of things you can do to make sure things go as smoothly as possible, which will give you the confidence to tackle longer trips alone.

• Plan your route before you go. If you are travelling by bus or train, make sure you know where you will be getting on or off.

• There are plenty of apps available to help you, with everything from times and prices to live updates if services are disrupted. It's a good idea to pop them on your phone so you can check it for any changes.

• When you get off at your stop, do you know how to get to the place you are visiting? Before you go, look up the address on an online map so you can see how far it is from your bus stop or train station. Some maps even drop you onto the street so you can really get your bearings. This way, when you step off the bus or train, you'll know exactly where you are heading.

• Some mobile phones also have maps so you can get directions as you are walking. But it's a good idea to have done some planning at home, just in case you can't get a signal.

• When you take a bus or train, be aware of who else is around you. Sit with other people if possible, rather than in a carriage by yourself.

• If you are travelling alone, let your parents and friends know which bus or train you are catching, what time you are expecting to arrive and when you will get home. If there are any problems and you are delayed, send them a text.

new street

green street

old street

• It's a good idea to have your final address and directions written down on paper too, not just in your phone. I've not done this on several occasions in the past, only to find my phone has battery died, leaving me with no idea of where I was supposed to be going or how to get there!

Ask Dr Christian

I don't feel safe on the bus...

Q: Last time I took the bus, this guy was acting really weird. Luckily I was with a friend, but if I'm alone, how can I keep myself safe?

A: If you find yourself in this sort of situation, then move seats. If you are upstairs, which can be more isolated, then move downstairs on the bus. If there is only one level, move to sit closer to other people or closer to the driver. If you are still being pestered then tell the conductor or driver as soon as possible. Don't wait for something nasty to happen before telling anyone.

WHEN THINGS DON'T GO TO PLAN...

Even when you've prepared for a trip, things don't always go entirely to plan. Here are some essential tips to help you cope when a journey goes a bit pear-shaped.

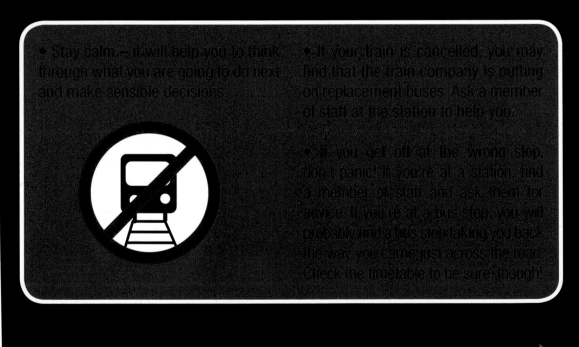

- Stay calm – it will help you to think through what you are going to do next and make sensible decisions.

- If your train is cancelled, you may find that the train company is putting on replacement buses. Ask a member of staff at the station to help you.

- If you get off at the wrong stop, don't panic! If you're at a station, find a member of staff and ask them for advice. If you're at a bus stop, you will probably find a bus stop taking you back the way you came just across the road. Check the timetable to be sure, though!

• Always carry your bus or train fare separately from your spending money so that you don't spend it and find you haven't got enough money for your ticket home.

• Carry some spare cash as 'emergency money' in case you lose your bus or train ticket.

• If you find yourself hopelessly lost or you've run out of money, don't be afraid to call your parents or another adult you trust. They will be glad that you asked for help if you are struggling to deal with something on your own.

• When you go out, make sure your mobile phone is charged up and that you have enough credit to make calls.

HOME ALONE

As you get older, it's likely that your parents may allow you to stay home alone for short periods. Here's how to stay safe:

• Make sure that you know when your parents or carers will be back and where they are. It's always useful to have a list of contact numbers that you can call if you need to. Have your parent's mobile number, plus the number of a relative or friend of the family to hand, just in case you need them.

• Keep the doors locked. If someone comes to the door, check who it is before you open it. If it is someone you know but you feel uneasy about letting them in, don't be afraid to tell them to come back later when your parents are home.

• If the phone rings, don't give out your name or any personal details. Caller ID is useful as you can use it to screen your calls. If a number comes up that you don't recognize, let the answerphone take it instead.

• Make sure you know how to phone the emergency services. The chances are you won't need to, but it's always best to be prepared.

Ask Dr Christian

My friend wants to throw a party in my house...

Q: My mum and dad are going out for the night and leaving me on my own for the first time. They've said I can invite my best friend over, but she's trying to persuade me to invite more people and throw a party. I don't want to lie to my parents, but I'll look stupid if I say no. What should I do?

A: Your parents are putting huge trust in you and making a very clear statement: that they think that you are sensible enough and grown up enough to look after yourself now. This is great news for you and may well be the start of your independence; being allowed to go out and about on your own more, or being allowed to stay on your own in the house overnight, and even with a friend. If you mess this up by having a party then you may well lose all of the trust that your parents have in you, and they will certainly not leave you alone again. I don't think you will look stupid if you tell your friend no: remember, it is not your house, it is your parents' house, and you must abide by their rules. Do the right thing this first time and you will find your parents will allow you more and more freedom. I think this is an easy choice for you to make.

TRAVELLING TO AND FROM SCHOOL

If you are starting secondary school soon, there will be plenty of new things to get to grips with. Not only will you be in a much bigger building, probably with a whole new set of people, you've also got to deal with getting there and back.

If you take the bus, you will notice quite quickly that there are a few unwritten rules such as who sits where. Rocking up in the first week of term and bagging yourself the back seat will not go down well with older year groups, so take a bit of time to work out who sits where and try to sit near people in your year group.

If you are walking to school, it's great to meet up with friends if you can and walk together. When walking alone, stick to busy streets and carry a charged mobile phone and some spare cash in case you need it. Try to use pedestrian or zebra crossings to cross roads, particularly if the roads are busy.

Cycling is a great way to get to and from school, if the route allows. Make sure you wear a helmet and cycle sensibly. Don't take chances – remember that a car may not be able to stop in time if you zip in front of them, which could result in a trip to A & E or worse. Take a decent bike lock with you and make sure you use it. The last thing you need after a busy day at school is to find that your wheels have been nicked!

Ask Dr Christian

I'm being bullied on the school bus...

Q: I love my new school but I'm finding the bus journey really tough. Some of the older kids have been picking on me and the other year 7s and I dread every morning. What should I do?

A: Being bullied anywhere can make life really miserable, and it is a real shame that you are enjoying your new school but dreading the journey there and back. On the school bus, try to sit near to the driver, or if it's an ordinary bus, by other adults. Remember that you can always tell your teachers at your school because, although you are not technically 'in' school when travelling, schools do have the power to punish bullies if the bullying happens on the way to and from school.

Ask Dr Christian

Should I lie to my parents...

Q: My friend wants me to get the train into the city with her. I know my parents will say no, but she's suggested I should just tell them I am going to her house. Should I lie to my parents and go?

A: Although sometimes it may be hard to work out what it is, your parents will have a reason for the rules and decisions they make. Not wanting you to go into the city is probably because it is easy to get lost in, and there are all sorts of risks and issues that you may not yet know how to deal with. Lying to your parents about where you are going can lead to huge problems. If something goes wrong, for example if you or they have an issue and need help or if they need to find you quickly, and you are not where you said you would be, this can cause huge delays, worry and distress for everyone. Not only that, but if your parents find out that you have been lying then they are very unlikely to trust you in the future or let you go anywhere else on your own again.

Ask Dr Christian

I don't want my phone to be stolen...

Q: One of my friends had his phone stolen on the way home from school. How can I make sure the same thing doesn't happen to me?

A: If you can, always try to walk home with friends, in a group. This makes it much harder for you to be singled out and picked on. Never walk down quiet, empty, unlit streets or alleyways on your own. It is also best to try and avoid using your phone when walking around on your own – if someone sees it, they might want to take it! Don't walk with headphones on as these may stop you from hearing

if anyone is approaching, and if you carry a bag, keep it in front of you where you can see it.

MAKE FRIENDS, BREAK FRIENDS

Sometimes, it can feel as if friendships have more ups and downs than a roller coaster. Almost overnight you can find that you don't have much in common with the people who were once your closest friends. Or, perhaps your one-time BFF is now hanging round with someone else and it is more than clear that you are not welcome. But here's something that no one ever tells you: friendships take work! Here's how to survive those ups and downs...

TAKE A CHANCE

When you are in a new situation, the thought of walking up and speaking to people you don't know can be terrifying. But remember that everyone feels the same and if you are brave, take a deep breath and say "Hi!" you might make some really amazing friends.

BE TRUE TO YOURSELF

By now, you probably have a good idea of who you are. You'll know what you like and don't like doing, as well as what sort of people you are drawn to. Never feel that you need to hide who you are so that people like you – real friends will like you for who you are and make you feel good about yourself.

COMMUNICATE

If you are upset with a friend, it may be tempting to sulk or give them the silent treatment, but this won't solve anything.

Talk to your friend and tell them how you feel. Rather than blaming them: "you were horrible to me..." try saying how you feel: "I felt hurt the other day when..." The chances are that your friend will be relieved you made the first move and you can resolve the upset and get over it.

TWO'S COMPANY...

If your BFF suddenly becomes close to someone else, you may find yourself feeling a bit sidelined. It's a horrible feeling, and it is hard to know how to deal with it. Try not to get too upset by it – use the chance to expand your friendship circle by spending time with other people.

IS IT YOU OR THEM?

Every school has them. The girl or guy that everyone looks up to. Good-looking, popular, brilliant at everything they do – no wonder everyone wants to be their friend. All too often, though, to stay at the top, the queen bee or top dog will need to put other people down. If they pick you, it can be awful. Whether they are the people you hang around with or just classmates, if they make you feel bad about yourself, leave you out or make you unhappy, it's easy to think there is something wrong with you. You might tell yourself that it's because you are not good enough, funny enough or clever enough to be around them. But resist the urge to start pulling yourself apart. Ask yourself if they are worth your time and energy – if they make you feel bad then steer well clear. Always remember: some people will dislike you because you are good at certain things, but others will like you for exactly the same reason. It is just a question of working out who is who.

WIDEN YOUR CIRCLE

If you are having friendship issues at school, one thing that can help you to manage it is by doing other things outside school. Whether it's sport, music, drama or photography, finding friends who share the same interests can really help to minimize the effect of school-friend dramas. It will also build your self-confidence, which is really important.

PEER PRESSURE

Have you ever felt like you had to do something you didn't like just to fit in? This could be anything from pretending that you like a particular band or TV show to playing a sport you're not keen on, right through to drinking, smoking or being mean to someone. This is known as 'peer pressure' and it means that you feel like you have to do something you don't feel comfortable doing just because your friends are doing it.

BE YOURSELF

Often, in a group of friends, you will find that there are one or two people who are strong characters and take the lead. Say, for example, that you are with your mates and one of them has brought along some cigarettes. He lights one and is pushing everyone to have a puff. But you don't want to. You hate smoking and you know how bad it is for you. On the other hand, you don't want to look silly or childish and you want your friends to like you. So should you try it, just to be the same as everyone else, or stick up for yourself?

BIG TROUBLE

It's not always easy to be the odd one out when a group of friends want to do something you're not comfortable with. But if you blindly follow the crowd, you are letting someone else decide what happens to you. At best, it means you might do some things that you wouldn't otherwise have done. At worst, it could mean that you find yourself in heaps of trouble. So, if people start pressurizing you to do something, remember that true friends don't make each other feel bad.

HOW TO SAY NO AND MEAN IT

An important part of self-confidence is learning how to say "no" when you're being pressured into doing something you don't want to do. This is called being assertive. It's not about being rude or aggressive – it's about knowing what you are comfortable with and being firm when someone tries to persuade you to do something you don't want to do. The best thing to do is to keep things short and simple: "No thanks, I don't want to do that," is fine. Your real friends will admire you for being strong and you could find that speaking out gives other friends the courage to say they don't want to do it either. It may feel scary, but remember that true friends will still like you if you stand up for yourself.

Ask Dr Christian

I saw my friend shoplifting...

Q: I've started hanging around with a new girl in my class. She's great fun, but last week when we went into town, I saw her steal some make-up. She's trying to persuade me to do it too, but my parents would go mad if I got caught. I don't want to lose her friendship, though, so what should I do?

A: You know what? It's not just your parents going mad at you that you need to worry about. If you get caught, you could end up having to talk to the police and may even end up having to go to a criminal court. Something like that can stick with you all your life. You don't do everything with your friend all the time do you? You live in separate places, have different parents, eat different food, quite possibly at different times. So you don't have to do everything together. If your friend is starting to do things that you know are not right, tell her – and if she still wants to do it, then walk away. You can either meet up with her later, or you may decide that she is not quite the friend that you thought she was. This can be very confusing and upsetting, but then so can being arrested for stealing.

60

Ask Dr Christian

People tease me for being Emo...

Q: People at school have started to tease me because I dress differently (I'm Emo). How do I deal with it?

A: I was stubbornly different at school. I hated sport, loved the theatre, and had very, very alternative tastes in music indeed. I also had a favourite jumper that I always wore, all the time, and always got teased for. But for one reason or another, I knew that I was just being me, doing the things that I wanted to do, and that I liked. And pretty soon, in time, the other kids realized that, well, that was just me. And there wasn't a lot that was going to change that! And so they got used to me, and we started to get on fine. Wear your clothes with pride, be confident about who you are and what you like, and soon people will realize that you have an identity that maybe, just maybe, they are a teeny bit jealous of!

MORE THAN FRIENDS...

Have you noticed that when a certain boy or girl is around, you get butterflies in your tummy and feel a bit awkward and clumsy? You may be desperate for them to notice you, but blush bright red if they so much as glance at you. These strong, exciting feelings are down to your hormones kicking in. They can make life very confusing sometimes, but don't worry, it is a perfectly normal part of growing up.

FANCYING SOMEONE

If you fancy someone, the first step is to get to know them properly. That way you can work out if you really like them and whether they fancy you back. The best way to start a conversation is by finding out what the person is interested in then finding a chance to chat to them about it. Don't be afraid to let them know you are interested in them – if they are too, great! If not, don't worry, it happens to all of us at some point. The best thing to do is to stay cool and move on!

FIRST DATES

If the person you fancy likes you too, the next step is a date. This might seem quite scary, but it needn't be if you keep it casual and low-key. If you feel more comfortable in a group, you could both ask some friends along.

FIRST KISSES

You may want to hold hands, hug or kiss on a date, and that's fine if you both feel ready. Listen to your own feelings and respect those of your date. You shouldn't feel pressured to do anything you don't want to, nor should you try to make your date do anything they don't want to either.

Ask Dr Christian

My ex is going out with my best friend...

Q: My boyfriend dumped me and I've just found out he is going out with my best friend. I feel so betrayed! What should I do?

A: This is definitely one of the more painful things that can happen in life. Falling in love with someone who doesn't love you back or, as in your case, falling for someone who then turns their attentions onto someone else can be agony. Whilst it may be tempting to phone them and text them all the time, or arrange 'chance' meetings with them, I would suggest that you try your hardest not to. You just need to give it time. The more time that passes, the less the pain will be and the more you will feel able to carry on with your life. And maybe, just maybe, somebody else will come to your attention who will quickly replace all thoughts of your last boyfriend. This may happen sooner than you think!

I suggest you talk to your best friend in a calm way and let her know how upset you feel. It's important to be be open and honest with your friends and not let resentments build up.

BULLYING

Bullying is horrible. It can involve anything from excluding someone to name-calling, teasing, hitting, pushing or kicking. Sometimes it can also involve being bullied online – you can find out more about cyberbullying on page 34. If you have ever been bullied, you will know how scary and lonely it can be. Bullying is a big deal and you should never feel like you have to cope with it on your own.

People bully for all sorts of reasons. Often or belittling other people, they can make it to because they feel unhappy about themselves feel better, or be powerful or like themselves and they think it to by making the popular.

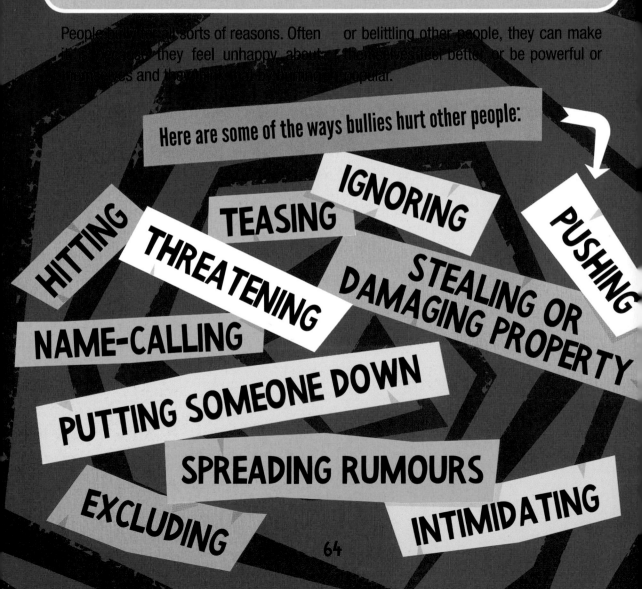

Here are some of the ways bullies hurt other people:

IGNORING

TEASING

HITTING

THREATENING

PUSHING

STEALING OR DAMAGING PROPERTY

NAME-CALLING

PUTTING SOMEONE DOWN

SPREADING RUMOURS

EXCLUDING

INTIMIDATING

Bullying is never OK. Don't feel like you need to deal with it on your own. Tell a trusted adult, such as a parent or teacher. It can help if you can keep a diary of things that are happening. If you are being sent nasty texts, emails or IMs, take screenshots, as these can all help to show people what has been happening. Every school has an anti-bullying policy to protect pupils so don't be afraid to speak up. If you think a friend is being bullied, don't be afraid to tell someone. No one has the right to bully other people or make them feel bad, so if you ever feel like being nasty, ask yourself how you would feel if the other person was behaving in the same way towards you. Be honest and ask yourself... are you being a bully?

Ask Dr Christian

I stood up to bullies and now they've turned on me...

Q: I stood up to some bullies who were hassling my friend. Now they've started bullying me, too. What can I do to stop it?

A: Well done for standing up to those bullies and for being brave enough to help your friend out. You know you have the guts to stand up to these sorts of people, but sometimes it can be difficult to get bullying to stop. If you get to a point where you feel unable to take any more or that it is getting out of control then remember, there are ALWAYS things you can do. Report the bullying to a teacher or someone at school you feel safe with. They may be able to take action and get the bullying to stop. If you are worried that it might make it worse, perhaps you can ask the teacher to just keep an eye on it as they then might see it themselves and take action. Tell a parent or a family member. This can give you lots of strength and a parent or family member can help you to get the bullying to stop. They can also give you lots of emotional support. It is important to try and tell someone in your family what is going on so you are not bottling things up. You could also try to ignore it and walk away. Quite often the bully stops when they are no longer receiving attention or a reaction. It is always difficult to try and ignore it, especially when it is so upsetting or if it is constant but if they don't get a reaction, it can stop.

Ask Dr Christian

My friends are excluding me...

Q: Since one of the girls in our class started hanging around with my group, I feel like my friends are excluding me. I'm not getting invites to stuff and they are being really off with me whenever I talk to them. They don't leave space for me at the lunch table and often they will walk off without me. I feel so alone. What can I do?

A: Clearly someone here (possibly the new member of the group) is influencing the others to turn against you and blank you. This must feel very upsetting, especially if you have no idea why it is happening. Sometimes it may be helpful to find a chance to talk to one of your old friends on their own, without the rest of the group around, to try to find out what is going on. Has someone been spreading rumours or gossiping about you? You could point out to your friend how you all used to get on well and how these rumours are spoiling things. She may see this is true and start to influence the rest of the group back towards you again. Or it may be time to start making new friends, to revisit people you used to hang out with more, and you may find that very quickly you have a new circle of mates who welcome you and support you, and you will not need to worry about your old clique anymore.

MONEY MANAGEMENT

You may be used to having a bit of cash in your pocket, either from an allowance or when you are given some birthday money. But what do you do with it? Are you a big spender or a super-saver? How do you get the balance right? Learning to manage your money is an important part of growing up and if you are savvy with your cash, you'll be able to make it stretch so you can do more of the things you enjoy with your mates.

FIRST JOBS

If you want to earn some extra cash, there are lots of ways to do it. From babysitting or chores around the house, to a paper round or doing odd jobs such as washing cars for family and neighbours. Ask around and see what you can do. I did a paper round as my first job. I had to get up horribly early and deliver the papers to all the local homes. Despite hating early mornings, I felt really grown up and independent doing it, and of course I loved the money it brought in, even if it was only a bit. This gave me even more of a sense of freedom and was, I suppose, the first step in not being totally reliant on my parents.

SELLING STUFF

If there are things you've grown out of or toys you don't play with any more, think about selling them to make some cash. Ask a parent to help you by putting an ad in the local paper or online. Alternatively, think about doing a car-boot sale with them.

GET CRAFTY

If you're creative, how about making jewellery, friendship bracelets or other items and selling them to your friends?

SPEND SOME, SAVE SOME

Going out and having fun with your mates is great, but it's a good idea to save some of the money you've earned. Open a savings account and make sure you add a little to it whenever you can. It's amazing how soon it adds up and it will be there for when you need it. Getting into the habit now means that when you are older you'll know how to manage your cash. Then you can plan for all the good things in life, like holidays and expensive treats, as well as being able to cover any unpleasant surprises like a big bill.

WHAT A BARGAIN!

Watch out for special offers or bargains. If you fancy a pizza with your mates, check online. Often there are discount vouchers and 2-for-1 offers so you can spend less and still have fun.

If you're shopping in the sales, don't be tempted to buy something just because it's a bargain. Be honest. Do you need it? Will you use it? Would you buy it if it was full price or are you just tempted as it is such a good deal? If the answer is no, put it back!

WHEN YOU'RE STRAPPED FOR CASH

Sometimes you can find yourself with friends who have lots more cash at their fingertips. You may feel pressured into trying to match their spends, whether it's expensive meals out, keeping up with all the latest fashions, or having the latest gadgets. Focusing on what they have and you don't is guaranteed to make you feel miserable and resentful. The truth is that real friends won't care whether you're having a movie night at home instead of an all-expenses-paid trip to Hollywood. Spending time together, not spending money is what counts. The best thing to do is be honest about your money, or lack of it. If you can't afford to do something, suggest something else that's cheaper or free. If your friends really want to spend time with you, they will understand and will want to do something you can all enjoy.

PERFECT PLANS

By now, some people will know exactly what they want to do when they grow up and have their whole lives mapped out, while other people won't have a clue what they are doing next week, let alone what they want to do in the future!

If you know what you want to do and how you are going to get there, that's great. If you're not sure, it's a good idea to start having a think about what your goals are and how you might go about achieving them. Jot down the things you are good at and think about how you could work them into your future.

Perhaps you are brilliant with computers and fancy working in programming or gaming. The next thing you need to do is to find out what you need to do to get there. If you are clear about your goals you can find out exactly what to do to make it happen.

 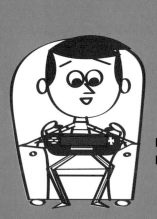 

Work hard at school, particularly in computer studies

Learn to code and play lots of computer games in your spare time

Become a successful computer programmer!

HOW WILL YOU GET THERE?

To work out what goals to set yourself, you'll need information. Often you can find out what you need to know by having a look online. Alternatively, if you know someone who's working in your dream job, ask them how they got there and what qualifications they have.

If you know you want to study medicine, for example, you'll need to make sure that you pick the right subjects to study when you choose your options. On the other hand, maybe you don't feel keen on an academic route. If you don't, there are plenty of other options open to you, such as doing an apprenticeship where you could learn anything from being a mechanic to hair and beauty.

The most important thing to remember when you are planning for your future is that life isn't a straight road. There will be lots of twists, turns and unexpected bumps on the way. You may get halfway to where you are going and decide that you want to change direction, and that's fine. The main thing to do is to make sure YOU are in the driving seat – if you really want something, you are far more likely to work hard to achieve it than if you are doing it just to please someone else. I thought I was going to end up a doctor working in a hospital all my life. That was the plan. And yet here I am now making TV shows and writing books for you. My life took an unexpected twist, and I love it. Just be ready to embrace and make the most of opportunities when they come along.

NEW EXPERIENCES

It might feel daunting, but try to see any new experience you have as an opportunity, whether it's moving to secondary school or starting a new job or club. Here's how to cope with new situations and new experiences:

IT'S OKAY TO FEEL SCARED

Moving school or trying something new can be daunting. Feeling scared is okay, as long as you manage it. Don't let your fear become so big that it stops you doing new things – after all, you never know what you might be missing!

CONFIDENCE

At parties and other social events, you may feel as if everyone else is more confident and outgoing than you are. The truth is that everyone finds social situations a bit scary, but some people have perfected the art of hiding their nerves and developed ways of coping. One of the keys to looking confident is the way that you hold yourself. Get it right and it sends out a positive vibe that says, 'Hey, I'm friendly and approachable!' Try it.

Hold your head up, unfold your arms, keep your shoulders back, make eye contact and smile! Even if you don't feel confident on the inside, you'll still look it on the outside. At first you might be faking it, but the more you practise this, the more confident you will feel.

WHAT IF I MAKE A FOOL OF MYSELF?

Everyone plays the 'what if' game. 'What if people laugh at me?' or 'what if no one likes me?', but you mustn't let these fears hold you back. Think about the worst that could happen. If you trip up and make a fool of yourself, does it really matter? You may feel a bit embarrassed, but this will only last for a short time. If you don't do anything because of what might happen, you may miss out on some truly amazing experiences.

BLUSHING

Social situations can seem all the worse if you find yourself blushing bright red as soon as someone looks your way. The good news is that it won't be half as obvious as it feels, even if your cheeks feel like they're on fire, and it will quickly pass. If you feel the familiar flush creeping up your face, take a moment to do some deep breathing – in for a count of four and out for a count of eight – which will relax you.

MAKE THE FIRST MOVE

Taking a deep breath and saying hello might seem scary, but it's the best way to break the ice with new people and you never know, the next person you approach may turn out to be a life-long friend! If you are struggling to think of something to say, ask the other person a question – you'll find that most people love the chance to talk about themselves.

EXPANDING YOUR SOCIAL GROUP

As you get older, you'll meet people from all sorts of cultures and backgrounds. Finding out about different cultures and beliefs can be really interesting – and there's no reason why two people with very different backgrounds and beliefs can't be very good friends, provided they respect each other and don't try to push their own views on the other person.

BEING WELL-ROUNDED

Think of the different things that make up your life: you, your family, friends, hobbies, schoolwork, health, physical activity and sleep, to name but a few. You need to give all of them attention. Spending every waking hour studying is just as unhealthy as spending all your time on your mates and ignoring everything else. The secret to being a well-rounded person is to give all the parts of your life attention and try to keep them balanced. Here's how:

BALANCE

To help your personality grow you must spend time on all parts of your life. So when you are at school this means trying your best, working hard and developing your skills. But what about after school and at weekends? It's just as important to spend quality time with your family and friends. Then of course there are hobbies and sports – whether you love art and karate or football and fencing, these are chances to try new skills as well as having lots of fun.

YOUR FUTURE SELF

There are many other ways to develop as a person. Your future self will thank you for the work you put in now.

STICK AT IT

Having a few hobbies that you keep doing for some time is great. It will show people that you are willing to try things, are a team-player and that you are reliable - all things that can help you if you are being interviewed for a college or uni place or a job. It can also help you learn new skills and make new friends.

TAKE AN INTEREST

Try and keep up with what's going on in the world - this doesn't mean reading all about your fave soap or reality TV programme - read up about current events and keep up to date with the news.

CHALLENGE YOURSELF

If your friend needs a running partner, or your local charity for the disabled needs volunteers, why not give it a go? You'll find you can achieve much more than you thought possible when you challenge yourself to try new things.

TRY IT OUT

If you already know what you want to do when you leave school, why not do some work experience? If it goes well, you may get invited back again, which gives you more practical skills in the role and it will look great on your CV!

STRESS-BUSTERS

COPING WITH STRESS

Everyone has times in their life when they feel worried. Usually it is down to something stressful that's happening in their lives, such as exams, arguments with friends or family, or having some really big issues to cope with. The good news is that there are lots of ways of coping when stress strikes.

EXAM WORRIES

Exams can be super-stressful at times, but there are plenty of things you can do to combat study stress.

GET ORGANIZED. If you leave studying until the night before your exam, you'll feel really panicky. Draw up a revision timetable and stick to it.

CREATE A STUDY SPACE. Find a quiet space where you won't be distracted by your family, the TV or the internet.

STUDY IN BURSTS. Our brains only have limited concentration spans, so try to have a break every 40 minutes or so. If it helps, set an alarm.

WHEN THE ALARM GOES, make yourself a drink or give yourself another reward such as ten minutes' surfing online. You need to be disciplined – when your break is up, get back to studying.

AT THE END OF THE DAY, treat yourself with something you really enjoy, whether it's watching a movie or seeing a friend. You've earned it!

ON THE DAY

THINK POSITIVE. Picture your exam going well – with all the preparation you've done, you can feel confident that you'll nail it.

KEEP CALM. It's natural to feel nervous, but don't let panic get the better of you. Close your eyes, take a deep breath in through your nose for a count of four and out through your mouth for a count of eight. After a few breaths, you'll be amazed at how relaxed you feel.

DO YOUR BEST. You've prepared well and you've gone into your exam calmly, so the only thing that's left to do is give it your best shot!

CATASTROPHIZING

One thing that's guaranteed to make a stressful situation feel even worse is if you start 'catastrophizing'. This is when you imagine all sorts of disastrous outcomes that are completely out of proportion to the real situation. For example, failing a maths exam may seem upsetting, but your life won't be over. You will still have options, such as resitting the exam, and you can use the experience to work out how to do better when you next take exams.

FAMILY

Every family is different. They can be big or small, you may have two homes if your parents live apart, or live with grandparents or foster parents. Love 'em or hate 'em, you spend most of your time with your family so learning how to get along and get through conflict is very important.

the Family
HOW TO GET ALONG

Living with other people, even those that you're related to, can be tough, especially if you feel like you don't get along. It's natural to have arguments in families, particularly as you may find you are starting to have very different ideas and opinions to your parents. It isn't always easy to express your own wishes and feelings, but learning to talk about things and to listen calmly can really cut down on the stress at home.

RESPECT
As you are becoming your own person with your own beliefs and opinions, you may find they are different to your parents. But learning to respect their wishes and feelings and seeing their point of view is very important.

PICK YOUR MOMENT
When tempers are short and emotions are running high, it's difficult to talk about things calmly and work out a solution. Ask to speak to the other person at a time when you are both feeling calmer and there aren't other distractions.

LEARN TO LISTEN

As well as talking and putting your own opinions across, it's important to let the other person speak – try to understand their point of view and find a compromise so you both feel happy.

CHOOSE YOUR WORDS CAREFULLY

Avoid blaming the other person: "you never let me go out with my friends," will make them feel far more defensive than if you talk about how you feel: "I felt upset when you wouldn't let me go to the sleepover."

SIBLINGS

Whether they're older or younger than you, siblings can be really irritating at times. If your siblings are annoying you, try to stay calm. Speak to your parents about it if you can. Remember to talk about how you feel, rather than how awful your sibling is being, as this will just rack up the tensions.

Some families may find that a good way to solve conflict is to have a family meeting every week. You can share good news, bad news and bring up any issues that are bugging you. Try to talk about them calmly using the tips above and left so that together you find a solution everyone is happy with.

SPACE

Space of your own in the family home is really important. Even if you share a room, try to make your 'side' a comfortable place where you can chill out. Keep it clutter-free and add a few bits and pieces like posters and photos to personalize it.

WHEN THINGS CHANGE...

If parents decide to split up and move apart, it can be very upsetting and you may feel quite mixed up about it. It's important to remember that it is not your fault and it is nothing you have done – it is the relationship between your parents that has changed, not their relationship with you.

If your parents are separated or divorced, you may split your time between two houses. It can be tricky to adjust to the different routines and rules in each. Try to talk about your feelings if you are finding things difficult. Sharing your worries with a trusted adult, a teacher or a counsellor can be very helpful in this situation.

BE KIND TO YOURSELF

Being well isn't just about looking after your physical health. It's also about looking after your emotional and mental health. A big part of this is to do with how you see yourself. This is called your 'self-esteem'. If you feel good about yourself and happy in your own skin, you are more likely to feel confident and positive. So how can you make sure your self-esteem is high?

THE GOOD, THE BAD AND THE UGLY Take a moment to jot down some things you like about yourself. There are no right or wrong answers, but you may have written things like 'funny', 'sporty' or 'clever'. If you take a moment to think, you probably have a few things you don't like about yourself, too.

THINK POSITIVE Sometimes it's easy to forget all the positive things about you and your life and spend your time focusing on the negatives. This can be very damaging to your confidence and your self-esteem. Next time you start thinking negatively, ask yourself if you are being too harsh and critical. Would you judge a friend the same way? Be kind to yourself and don't ignore all the positives to focus on one tiny negative.

BUILD ON SUCCESSES:

When something goes really well, spend a while thinking about why it was good. So for example, say your friend asks you to try out a new sport with him. You are really nervous and can't decide whether to go, but he persuades you, so you decide to be brave and give it a try. To your surprise you love it and find you are really rather good at the sport. Even though you felt scared, you overcame your negative feelings. You went in with a positive, open mind and it went well, so next time you'll feel even more confident about giving something new a go.

DON'T BE AFRAID TO FAIL:

Imagine that you go along to try a new sport and you hate it. It's easy to start being negative: "I'm rubbish, I don't know why I bothered..." and so on. Instead of getting into a unhelpful spiral of negative thoughts where you convince yourself that you are a terrible person, remember that just because something didn't go as planned, it doesn't change who you are. Instead you should be pleased that you were brave enough to try – not everyone likes the same thing and there will be other sports that are more suited to you that you will enjoy more. It's only by being brave and trying things that we find out who we are and what works (and doesn't work) for us. Accept it wasn't for you and move on.

MOOD-BUSTERS

Do you find there are days when you wake up feeling grumpy and snappy for no reason? You can't put into words why you feel this way, but you feel so on edge that the smallest thing that goes wrong is enough to make you explode with rage.

If you ever feel like this, the chances are that you just want to curl up under your duvet and be left alone. The trouble is you can't... you've got school and that means you somehow have to get through the day without screaming at someone or falling out with your best friend.

When you are feeling like this, one of the best ways to get it out of your system is by doing something physical, whether it is going for a run, punching a pillow or punchbag, or even just going for a walk. Whenever we exercise, our bodies release feel-good hormones, so something as simple as this can be enough to make the bad mood melt away.

WHEN ANGER STRIKES

You may also be finding that you feel really angry about things – far more than you used to. When you lose your temper, it can be pretty difficult to cool down again. You may feel so full of fury that you can't think straight. So how can you get your feelings under control?

Everyone has their own way of dealing with anger. The trick is finding what works for you, whether it is spending some quiet time alone to calm down, or doing some exercise to release all the fury you feel. The other thing that can really help is by doing some deep breathing. Close your eyes and breathe in through your nose for a count of four and out through your mouth for a count of eight. Repeat this until you feel a sense of calm returning.

BEATING THE BLUES

Everyone gets down sometimes – that's normal, especially if you are dealing with some stressful things. If you find you start to feel low all the time or stop going out and lose interest in daily life, it may be that you are depressed. Many people believe that children and teenagers can't have depression, but it is more common than people think. Thankfully attitudes towards depression have changed a lot over the last few decades so if you are feeling low, never be afraid to talk to people such as your parents or your GP – it's just as important to look after your mental health as it is to look after your physical health.

PANIC!

You're in a stressful situation. You can feel the blood rushing around your ears and your heart hammering. Your throat feels like it is closing up and you can't breathe. Sounds terrifying – and you might even convince yourself that you are dying, but what's most likely is that you are having a panic attack. This happens when your body goes into overdrive and floods with loads of stress hormones telling you, "this is really scary and dangerous, run away now!" It can make you feel awful, but many people have them at some point in their lives. And the good news is that there are many counsellors who can help you to deal with panic attacks and put coping strategies in place for when they happen. Speak to your GP and they will be able to put you in touch with someone who can help you overcome them.

SELF-HARM

Sometimes teenagers who are feeling low or bad about themselves will cut or harm themselves in other ways. Although they may feel that it provides an outlet to help them cope with difficult feelings and situations, it can be very dangerous. Try to confide in a trusted adult if you can, or call one of the helpline numbers in the back of this book – never feel that you have to cope with any problems on your own; there are always people there who can listen and help. Together you can identify the triggers that make you want to self-harm and find healthy ways of coping with them.

Ask Dr Christian

I feel sad all the time...

Q: I feel really down and have done for some time. I've stopped seeing my friends and I don't want to do anything. What should I do?

A: I think you need to talk to someone. Start with your parents, or, if you don't feel so comfortable with them, a close friend or even a teacher. Tell them how you are feeling and the sorts of thoughts that you have been having. You may feel reluctant to do this because of your mood, or because you think your problems aren't important enough, but really try to make yourself as it will give you some important insights into what is going on. Together you may be able to work out why you feel this way, or there may be no obvious reason at all. As you get more used to talking about your feelings, the next step would be to see your GP to talk through your thoughts with them. They can offer you specific help depending on their assessment of you. Whilst you may feel now like there is no way out and nothing will ever change, I can promise you that once you start talking and getting treatment, things will quickly improve.

TALK IT OUT

When you have a problem, it can be really helpful to have someone to talk about it with. You might confide in your mum, your gran, or perhaps you have a BFF who you share everything with. Talking it through can make a problem seem easier to cope with. You can work out how to deal with it, explore your feelings about it – sometimes it's enough just to be able to share it and have a good old moan!

Choosing who to talk to about stuff is really important. You've probably got a couple of good friends who you feel you can share anything with. That's great, but before you confide any big things to them, see how they deal with any minor stuff you tell them about. If you start to hear that other people know about it, it may be that your friends aren't quite as trustworthy as you thought! Good friends don't break a confidence, so make sure you are choosy about who you share stuff with.

As well as your friends, there are plenty of other people you can talk to. You might feel a bit funny talking about some stuff with your parents, but do give it a try. They will do their best to help you, and if you feel you can't open up to them totally, they may be able to help you find someone else to talk to, like a counsellor. You can also talk to an older sibling, a trusted teacher or another health professional.

Remember that anything you say to a health professional is confidential, too, so don't be afraid to talk to them openly and honestly. If you prefer, there are also helplines you can call (see page 92), where you can speak to someone anonymously without worrying that they will judge you or tell anyone else.

WHEN A PROBLEM IS TOO BIG...

Every so often, you may find that a friend shares a really big problem with you and swears you to secrecy. The trouble is it's *sooo* big that you're not sure how to deal with it on your own. You might feel overwhelmed by it, or helpless, because you've never dealt with anything like it before. Being trustworthy and able to keep a secret is very important if you are a good friend, but do remember that if a problem is very serious then you may need to break a confidence to be able to help your friend deal with whatever is happening.

If you can speak to a parent about it, that's great. They will be pleased that you have told them and will be able to talk you through what options there are to help your friend. Alternatively you could talk to a trusted teacher or call one of the helplines at the back of this book. Let your friend know that you have spoken to someone on their behalf. At first, they may be upset that you have told someone else, but if they are trying to cope with a serious situation on their own, they will be glad to have proper support.

88

Ask Dr Christian

I'm really worried about my friend...

Q: I'm really worried about my friend. She is a carer for her disabled mum. She's often away from school and is struggling with schoolwork and looking after her younger brothers and sisters. How can I help her? I don't want to get her in trouble with Social Services – I'm afraid they will break up the family, but my friend is really down and exhausted.

A: Your friend needs to know that she should not have to deal with these sorts of problems on her own. She really does need some adult help. Telling an adult doesn't mean that Social Services will then break up her family – it's more likely that they will be able to provide some help for her mother so that your friend can keep attending school. This is very important. I think you should chat to your friend about it and decide between you who would be the best person to tell. Maybe a favourite teacher at school, or your parents? They can then decide who to go to next.

Ask Dr Christian

I just get so angry...

Q: Sometimes when I'm angry I feel like my body is taken over by a monster. It's like I'm completely out of control. I say horrible things, slam doors and even throw stuff! Afterwards, I feel terrible about it. What should I do?

A: Anger is a normal, healthy emotion. But it sounds like you are having difficulty managing your anger and keeping it under control. The first step is to recognize when these angry feelings are building up and start taking steps to calm yourself down. Your heart usually beats faster and you breathe more quickly, preparing for action. You might also notice other signs, such as tension in your shoulders or clenching your fists. If you notice these signs, then you should try to get out of the situation before it gets out of hand. Try counting to 10. This gives you time to cool down so you can think more clearly and overcome the impulse to lash out. Breathe slowly. Breathing out for longer than you breathe in and relaxing as you breathe out will calm you down effectively and help you think more clearly. Once you're able to recognize the signs that you're getting angry and can calm yourself down, you can start looking at ways to control your anger more generally. Bringing down your general stress levels with exercise and relaxation is important. Make sure you are getting enough sleep, and talk through any worries you may have instead of keeping them all to yourself. Other people can help you too, so if you feel you are not able to control it, then ask your GP for some help.

Ask Dr Christian

I feel really down in winter...

Q: Every winter, I feel really low and tired. My dad mentioned SAD. What is it and how do I know if I have it?

A: Seasonal affective disorder (SAD) is a type of depression that has a seasonal pattern, with episodes occurring at the same time each year, usually during the winter. The main symptoms are a low mood and a lack of interest in life. You may also be less active than normal and sleep more. These symptoms often begin in the autumn as the days start getting shorter. They're most severe during December, January and February, and in most cases the symptoms of SAD begin to improve in the spring before eventually disappearing. I think that you should visit your GP as you do seem to have the symptoms of SAD. They may carry out an assessment to check your mental health. If they also think that you may be affected then they can go through various treatment options with you. Light therapy is often used to treat SAD and involves sitting in front of or beneath a light box that produces a very bright light. Light boxes come in a variety of designs, including desk lamps and wall-mounted fixtures.

To find out more about all the topics we've covered, turn the page for some useful resources.

RESOURCES

STAYING HEALTHY:

www.gosh.nhs.uk
(UK site)
General health advice produced by the experts at Great Ormond Street Hospital (GOSH). It's packed with top tips to help you lead a more active and healthy lifestyle as you grow up into an adult. Find information on how to improve your diet, the benefits of doing regular exercise and advice on looking after your mental health.

www.kidshealth.org
(US site)
If you're looking for information you can trust about kids and teens that's free of 'doctor speak', you've come to the right place. KidsHealth is the most-visited site on the web for information about health, behaviour and development from before birth through the teen years.

www.girlshealth.gov
(US site)
The mission of girlshealth.gov is to promote healthy, positive behaviours in girls between the ages of 10 and 16. Girlshealth.gov gives girls reliable, useful information on the health issues they will face as they become young women, and tips on handling relationships with family and friends, at school and at home.

www.healthykids.nsw.gov.au
(Australian site)
A 'one-stop shop' of information for parents and carers, teachers and childcare workers, health and other professionals and kid and teens about healthy eating and physical activity.

STAYING SAFE ONLINE:

www.childnet.com/young-people

The internet is an amazing place and a wonderful resource and the aim of this site is to help make it a great and safe place for children and young people. Find the latest information on the sites and services that you like to use, plus information about mobiles, gaming, downloading, social networking and much more.

www.thinkuknow.co.uk

Come in to find the latest information on the sites you like to visit, mobiles and new technology. Find out what's good, what's not and what you can do about it. If you look after young people there's an area for you too – with resources you can use in the classroom or at home. Most importantly, there's also a place which anyone can use to report if they feel uncomfortable or worried about someone they are chatting to online.

www.kidsmart.org.uk

Kidsmart is an award-winning practical internet safety programme website for schools, young people, parents, and agencies, produced by the children's internet charity Childnet International.

BULLYING:

www.nobullying.com

Nobullying.com is an online forum aimed at educating, advising, counselling and all importantly, helping to stop bullying, in particular, cyber bullying.

www.beatbullying.org

BeatBullying is an international bullying prevention charity working and campaigning to make bullying unacceptable, on the ground in the UK and across Europe. They believe that no one should endure the pain, fear or isolation of being bullied, and that everyone has the right to be safe from bullying, violence and harassment. BeatBullying stops bullying and keeps young people safe.

GENERAL ADVICE:

www.childline.org.uk
You can talk to ChildLine about anything. Whether you're feeling stressed, anxious, lonely or down – they are there for you. Their counsellors help lots of young people with all sorts of things, like bullying, problems at home and self-harm. Whatever it is, they can help. ChildLine is a private and confidential service, meaning that what you say stays between you and ChildLine. Call free on 0800 1111. Calls are confidential and won't appear on the phone bill, including mobiles.

www.bbc.co.uk/radio1/advice
Helping you get through life. Categories include: Sex & Relationships; Drink & Drugs; Bullying; Studying & Work; Your Body; Your Health & Wellbeing; Money, Law & Your World

www.likeitis.org
Likeitis gives young people access to information about all aspects of sex education and teenage life.

ALCOHOL AND DRUGS:

www.talktofrank.com
Friendly, confidential drugs advice.

INDEX